Peyt

The Inspirational Story of Football Superstar Peyton Manning

Copyright 2015 by Bill Redban - All rights reserved.

This document is geared towards providing exact and reliable information in regards to the topic and issue covered. The publication is sold with the idea that the publisher is not required to render accounting, officially permitted, or otherwise, qualified services. If advice is necessary, legal or professional, a practiced individual in the profession should be ordered.

In no way is it legal to reproduce, duplicate, or transmit any part of this document in either electronic means or in printed format. Recording of this publication is strictly prohibited and any storage of this document is not allowed unless with written permission from the publisher. All rights reserved.

The information provided herein is stated to be truthful and consistent, in that any liability, in terms of inattention or otherwise, by any usage or abuse of any policies, processes, or directions contained within is the solitary and utter responsibility of the recipient reader. Under no circumstances will any legal responsibility or blame be held against the publisher for any reparation, damages, or monetary loss due to the information herein, either directly or indirectly.

The information herein is offered for informational purposes solely, and is universal as so. The presentation of the information is without contract or any type of guarantee assurance.

The trademarks that are used are without any consent, and the publication of the trademark is without permission or backing by the trademark owner. All trademarks and brands within this book are for clarifying purposes only and are owned by the owners themselves, not affiliated with this document.

Table Of Contents

Introduction

Chapter 1: Born for the Position

Chapter 2: Game's On

Chapter 3: Manning the Field

Chapter 4: Off the Field

Chapter 5: The Big Heart of the Big Name

Chapter 6: The History Made

Conclusion

Introduction

As the title already implies, this is a book about [The Inspirational Story of Football Superstar Peyton Manning] and how he rose from his life in the New Orleans area to becoming one of today's leading and most-respected football players. In his rise to superstardom, Peyton Manning has inspired not only the youth, but fans of all ages throughout the world.

This book also portrays the struggles that Peyton Manning had to overcome during his early childhood years, his teen years, and even up until he became what he is today. A notable source of inspiration is Manning's own Foundation, which is named after him, and his consistent support of other charitable organizations, such as the Boys and Girls Foundation, as well as numerous others. He continues to serve as the humble, mild-mannered superstar in a sport that glorifies flashy plays and mega personalities.

Combining incredible accuracy, quick decision-making, nimble feet, and superior coordination, Peyton has shown the ability to slice up just about any kind of defense. From being Archie Manning's kid to becoming, perhaps, the greatest offensive player of his generation, you'll learn here how this man has risen to the ranks of the best football players of all-time.

Thanks again for downloading this book, I hope you enjoy it!

Chapter 1:

Born for the Position

"I had a very supportive childhood; had two great parents that loved me, supported me, hugged me after games, win or lose." –Peyton Manning

On March 24, 1976, Peyton Williams Manning was born in New Orleans, Louisiana. He is the second son of Archie and Olivia Manning; Cooper is the oldest son in the family, born in 1974, while Eli, the youngest, arrived in 1981.

The Manning brothers are said to have been born for athletics, which was readily apparent from the moment they learned how to crawl. This may not be surprising, considering the genes they carry in them. Their father, Archie Manning, was well-known for his impressive career as the New Orleans Saints' quarterback in the National Football League from 1971 to 1982.

The love for sports comes naturally to Peyton and his brothers. Although their father was a renowned professional football player, he never forced any of his kids to be inclined towards sports. Nevertheless, once his support was needed, he was always more than willing to give professional and fatherly guidance. Thus, Peyton believes that his passion for football emanated from the essential lessons learned from his father.

Another source of inspiration and mentoring was provided by Peyton's older brother, Cooper. As a wide receiver, Cooper excelled in football during his high school years, and was recruited heavily by Division I-A schools. However, Cooper's plan - regarding his professional football career - ended when he was diagnosed with a congenital medical condition called spinal stenosis. Since having a career in sports was no longer a possibility, Cooper opted to develop a business after graduating from college.

As early as 3 years of age, Peyton started throwing the pigskin around with his brother, Cooper. Indeed, Peyton's early childhood started to polish his deep love for football. His father's fame and their well-kept family values provided a very supportive and motivating social environment for the growing Peyton and his siblings. The kind of parenting Archie and Olivia provided was successful at positively influencing the attitudes of their children.

As a child, Peyton watched his father closely. He was keen on observing how his father handled his professional career, how he dealt with the media, and even with fans after the games. Despite the love and passion for sports, Peyton never thought he would someday be doing things that his father was doing as a professional football player. Nonetheless, now that he has ended up in a similar situation, everything he saw in Archie's professional life has helped shape him into the person he is today.

As a kid, Peyton was described as a sweet and protective kind of person. He never liked it when he saw someone that was taking advantage of another person. Also, as a child, Peyton was a tedious youngster. He made his bed, checked and re-checked the door locks, and liked things to be organized.

In school, Peyton was a grinder; he worked hard to get the best grades that he could possibly get. He's described himself as a "preparation guy", which, until now, still defines his style. He was the type that might not stay up late studying for a test, but would, instead, get up at 5 in the morning to prepare for school.

These days, Peyton is admired - not just by fans, but also by professionals - for his work ethic. Now that we know his childhood, we can see that the development of his work ethic has been something that has evolved over his lifetime. Peyton was taught to have a strong work ethic early in his childhood. He would seek advice, mostly from his father, then, and even now as an All-Pro quarterback. During Peyton's childhood, Archie used to give him different quotes cut from the newspaper, or taken from a quote book. These inspirational quotes served their purpose, adding more motivation for the growing Peyton.

In 1982, Archie Manning was traded to the Houston Oilers, forcing him to leave the family in New Orleans for a little while. Two years afterwards, Olivia and the kids followed Archie to Minneapolis for his last season in the NFL Peyton was too young for the fifth grade squad, thus missing the chance to play organized football in Minneapolis.

Peyton in High School

The Mannings returned to New Orleans a year later and Peyton entered secondary education at Isidore Newman School. Unfortunately for Peyton, who was looking forward to playing football in his new school, Newman cancelled the football program for the sixth grade.

Nonetheless, the time for Peyton to put on his pads at last came in 1988. Peyton started three consecutive seasons as quarterback for coaches Tony Reginelli and Keefe Hecker in Isidore Newman School.

Archie was with the New Orleans Saints as a star quarterback when Peyton was attending high school. During the off-season practices for the Saints, Peyton, together with his two brothers, would tag along. Luckily, as early as 15 years of age, Peyton was allowed, by coach Jim Mora, to join workouts and even throw routes to Saints receivers.

Archie later said that he was not purposely trying to expose his kids to football during those practice days. He just wanted to spend time with his boys.

Peyton was not just all about having the stamina and strength to keep up with highly professional players at a young age - learning was very important for him. He was fond of watching films of professional games; he meticulously studied game plays and techniques.

Looking back, this is not surprising, considering that he has become known famously for the extreme preparation that he goes through before facing an opponent in a game.

Among the highlights of Peyton's high school career was winning the Gatorade Circle of Champions National Player of the Year award, New Orleans Quarterback Club Player of the Year, and the Nation's High School Offensive Player of the Year by Columbus (Ohio) Touchdown Club, to name a few, as well as completing 168 of 265 passes for 2,703 yards as a senior.

Peyton Goes to College

With such achievements, it was just logical for Peyton to receive twenty-three calls from different colleges in August of 1993. Aside from having too many options to choose from, there was also the pressure for Peyton to attend the University of Mississippi, his father's Alma Mater.

However, Archie never interfered with Peyton's decision making, despite having a lot of unsolicited advice from friends that he must make his son attend Ole Miss. In 1994, Peyton decided to sign the letter-of-intent to play for the University of Tennessee Volunteers.

Chapter 2:

Game's On

"I think experience is the best teacher in all facets, and so to play college football in a place like Tennessee, extremely high-profile program, playing on national TV every Saturday, great big crowds and demands on your time as a student athlete, I think that experience prepared me as much as it could for the professional ranks." - Peyton Manning

Peyton's hard-working attitude continued as he entered college: He arrived 6 weeks before the football camp to start his personal workouts. In his first year, Peyton was named the S.E.C. Freshman of the Year. Even in the off-seasons, Peyton never stopped working to become better and better each and every day. He watched videos of professional games and worked to improve his footwork and strength, as well as organizing unofficial practices with the key players on his team. Not a day was wasted for Peyton, who was determined to win every week.

In the fall of 1995, Peyton became Tennessee's leader. He led the team to a record of 10-1 and then finished at #2 in the polls, as the team handled Ohio State in the Citrus Bowl. Peyton completed 244 of 380 passes for 22 touchdowns. He received several All-Academic awards after the season ended. Moreover, he was awarded second-team All-Conference by the Associated Press (AP) and Coaches' All-S.E.C. first-team pick.

However, it was not always sunny for Peyton Manning during his collegiate career. In a meat-grinding S.E.C. game, the Volunteers collapsed in the final quarters, and the campaign was viewed as a total failure, in a loss to the University of Florida. Indeed, Peyton's college career was full of successes and failures, but being the fighter that he was (and still is), he never lost his heart in the game.

Over his four-year collegiate career, Peyton was able to set an astonishing 42 conference, NCAA, and school records. In an overall count, Peyton was able to execute the following: Passed for 11,201 yards, 863 completions, and 89 touchdowns. During his freshman year, he was able to throw for three touchdowns against

South Carolina. As a sophomore, Peyton logged his first 300-yard game against Georgia. Peyton's first 400-yard game was recorded when he was in his junior year, in a game against Florida, and as a senior, he showcased his first 500-yard day, throwing against Kentucky. Also, for his college career, Peyton charted the lowest interception percentage of all-time: Only 33 interceptions in 1,381 attempts, which accounts for only 2.39%.

At the age of 21, Peyton astonished the football realm by passing up the chance to go professional. The star quarterback of the Tennessee Volunteers opted to stay another year in school, to continue his studies and develop his game even further.

In 1998, Peyton graduated with a bachelor's degree in Speech Communications and was given prominent awards, like the Phi Beta Kappa honors, as well as the sought-after Sullivan Award - an honor given not just for excelling in athletic performance, but also in leadership and character. Other awards Peyton received include the Maxwell Trophy for college football's best player, and the Davey O'Brien and Johnny Unitas awards as the nation's best passer.

Having a college education was very significant for Peyton, and this perspective was strengthened even more after what happened to his older brother, Cooper. He became fully aware of the bitter reality that a football career could vanish in one play.

Thus, he really worked hard to earn his college degree, even while maintaining his professional aspirations. With his degree, he felt that he could be certain that he could succeed elsewhere if his football career failed.

Chapter 3:

Manning the Field

"One thing that can never be sacrificed is your preparation and your work ethic." - Peyton Manning

With the first overall pick in the NFL draft, Manning, in 1998, was selected by the Indianapolis Colts. His beginning years, however, were filled with ups and downs. Glorious moments were usually followed by struggles. Still, with hard-work and an operative work ethic, Peyton's professional life started to reach a level of accomplishment fundamentally unmatched in the league's history.

The next 13 years of Manning's dominance in the NFL allowed him to reap the fruits of all his hard work and professionalism. He has been awarded the Most Valuable Player, not just once or twice, but four times (2003, 2004, 2008, and 2009). Such a record was a first in the history of the NFL He is also noted for having the record of being the fastest to have achieved 4,000 completions, and pass for 50,000 yards.

There are some people that say that Peyton, despite having astonishing achievements, cannot actually win the big game. Peyton, who made twelve appearances in the Pro Bowl, answered critics by leading his team to win Super Bowl XLI in 2007.

Peyton is not just a voracious football superstar. There is also a side of him, off the field, that people love as well. He has starred in funny television commercials for Gatorade, MasterCard, and Sprint. Moreover, he has hosted Saturday Night Live.

Peyton was actually in so many commercials that there were often jokes about Peyton Manning being in every commercial you watch. Sometimes between an NFL game's commercial break, you could see 2 out of 5 commercials with Peyton Manning as the featured star.

In 2011, Peyton underwent surgery to repair damaged nerves in his neck, which was weakening his throwing arm. The spinal fusion performed on him caused him to miss the season and even cut short his stint with the Colts. The following year, Peyton signed a five-year contract, worth $96 million, with the Denver Broncos.

On February 2, 2013, Peyton was presented with the AP National Football League Comeback Player of the Year award. Also, Peyton was able to establish a new record in the history of the NFL, as the very first quarterback to make the Pro Bowl after missing the previous season due to injury.

Unfortunately, in his first season back, the Broncos lost 38-35 to Baltimore, who was the eventual winner of Super Bowl XLVII. Despite not winning the game, the Broncos, after the 2012 season, became the third team to win 11 consecutive games by at least a single touchdown, in NFL history.

Chapter 4:

Off the Field

"Love is a pretty commonly used word in our family." - Peyton Manning

Peyton is fortunate enough to have a healthy family relationship, which has helped him develop strong character as an individual, and as a professional. Although sports was naturally intertwined with the Mannings, they still have ample time to enjoy a life away from the field.

In 2000, Peyton and Archie Manning co-authored a book entitled, *Manning: A Father, His Sons, and a Football Legacy.* The book revolves around the father and son's lives, careers, and perspectives on football. Peyton's writing skill was once again showcased when he, Eli, and Archie wrote another book for children, which was called *Family Huddle*. Featured in this book are some childhood pictures of the Manning brothers playing football at an early age.

Peyton also has had several appearances on television. Hosting *Saturday Night Live* on his 31st birthday gave the show the highest household rating in more than 10 months. In 2009, Peyton and his brothers, Eli and Cooper, guest-voiced on an episode of *The Simpsons,* entitled, "O Brother, Where Bart Thou?"

In 2001, Peyton married Ashley Thompson, whom he met during his freshman year at the University of Tennessee. Ashley soon gave birth to twins, a girl and a boy, Mosley and Marshall William.

The success of Peyton's career has, at times, overshadowed his younger brother Eli's career. Many times during Eli's struggles at the beginning of his career in New York, Peyton would be asked by the media if Eli could ever be successful in the league. Peyton has always been extremely protective of Eli and wouldn't allow anyone to insult or disrespect Eli's playing career.

Peyton even attends Eli's big games, including the 2 Super Bowls that he has won with the New York Giants. In both the games, Peyton was sitting with family and cheering on Eli to win the game. It is fair to say that, despite the competitive nature of both Eli and Peyton, there is a strong desire for the other's success. The only time they don't want the other to win, is when they are facing each other in a game.

The media has often called games between Eli and Peyton, the "Manning Bowl", and each game has received very high ratings in terms of viewers.

Many people have also called Peyton the NFL's most marketable player. This is very rare for a player on a small market team, as he was when he was playing for the Indianapolis Colts.

Chapter 5:

The Big Heart of the Big Name

"I'm proudest of some of the work that we've done off the field..." - Peyton Manning

Obviously, Peyton Manning is a big name in the sports realm. Aside from the physical gifts, standing 6'5" and weighing 230 lbs., and having an admirable attitude and work ethic, there is something even more attracting about this legendary quarterback: He is well known for having a big heart, as well.

In 1999, Peyton established the PeyBack Foundation, which is aimed at providing grants to programs that can offer growth and leadership opportunities to children at risk in Tennessee, Indiana, and Louisiana (particularly in New Orleans). These three states are the ones that made a huge impact on Peyton, and for him, starting the foundation is simply "paying back" for all the blessings he has received, and for the undying support from his fans who reside there.

The PeyBack Foundation caters support for sports programs, field trips for children at-risk, academic coaching, book distribution, individual donations to homeroom teachers for special projects, and food and clothing for needy families. The foundation has helped 147 youth organizations by providing $800,000 in grants, with $100,000 given to court-appointed child-advocate programs of Marion County, Indiana, for abused children.

In addition to this, Peyton provides 800 Thanksgiving meals to less fortunate families, and allocates $40,000 in college scholarships every year.

In 2007, St. Vincent Health, an Indianapolis hospital, received an undisclosed donation from Peyton, and as a sign of gratitude, the hospital was renamed the Peyton Manning Children's Hospital at St. Vincent. As of 2009, Peyton's foundation has provided over $500,000 to help over 100 community organizations.

These are just some of the noble deeds Peyton has been doing since 1999. He is blessed and he is more than willing to share his blessings with other people. There are numerous writings, news, and testimonials talking about how people's lives were touched by the superstar quarterback, and there are plenty more that are not covered by the mass media.

According to people who have received help from Peyton, what makes him more admirable and respectable is the fact that he does not like any grandiose credit for the help that he is doing—a genuine act of kindness and humility indeed. Today we can think of only a handful of celebrities who are offering help without the flashing cameras of the media in front of them.

Still, Peyton's work with the PeyBack Foundation was greatly acknowledged, thus he received the Samuel S. Beard Award for Greatest Public Service by an Individual 35 Years or Under. It is not just within the realm of football that Manning is gathering trophies.

A particular teacher wrote a letter to Peyton and told him how her students, who were involved in the PeyBack Foundation, as well as some other programs of Peyton's, are performing better in class, primarily because they feel that someone is looking out for them. This is just one of the many stories showing how people, especially young ones, are inspired and motivated by Peyton. Being a football superstar is one thing, but being a person with a heart for everyone else is another. Peyton is admired not only because he is good in what he does professionally, but also because of his character and good heart off the field.

In 1998, Peyton opened the Manning Passing Academy to help aspiring athletes further enhance their skills. Patrick Ramsey, a former starting quarterback for the Washington Redskins, is a known graduate of Peyton's academy. The reason for his academy's success can be traced to the fact that Peyton serves as an inspiration for several individuals. How he manages his personal and professional life is something people are looking up to; he is well-respected in his field of expertise, and he is admired as a citizen outside the field as well.

Chapter 6:

The History Made

"Pressure is something that you feel only when you don't know what you're doing." - Chuck Noll

There are several things that have helped Peyton accomplish his remarkable achievements. Alongside the family and community support is wisdom passed down as quotes that have guided Peyton through his journey on the football field. One particular quote was from Chuck Noll, and is stated above.

Here are some of the major highlights and career milestones for the renowned quarterback.

High School Awards

Louisiana Class 2A MVP (1992 and 1993)

Gatorade High School Player of the Year (National – 1993)

New Orleans Quarterback Club Player of the Year (1993)

College Awards

S.E.C. Freshman of the Year (1994)

Maxwell Award (1996)

James E. Sullivan Award (1996)

S.E.C. Championship MVP (1997)

Citrus Bowl MVP (1997)

S.E.C. Player of the Year (1997)

NFL Awards

NFL MVP (2003, 2004, 2008, 2009)

Best NFL Player ESPY Award (2004, 2005)

Bert Bell Award (2003, 2004)

AFC Offensive Player of the Year Award (1999, 2003, 2004, 2005, 2008, 2009, 2012)

Pro Bowl MVP (2005)

Super Bowl MVP (2007)

NFL Comeback Player of the Year (2012)

Manning in the National Football League

Peyton Manning's training and hard work from high school to college prepared him for his professional career. He is the type of person that wants to be better and perform better every game; thus, he never wasted time and, instead, continued working to be the best quarterback that he could be.

With hard work and innate abilities, Peyton was able to accomplish a number of individual records, which include the following:

115 regular season wins as a starting QB in a decade

124 regular and postseason wins as a starting QB in a decade

Most AP NFL MVP Awards: 4

314 Touchdown Passes in a decade

42,254 Passing Yards in a decade

3,575 Completions in a decade

23 consecutive regular season wins as a starter

Only QB with seven straight seasons of 12+ wins as a starter

Only QB with nine straight seasons of 10+ wins as a starter

Only QB to lead five consecutive 4th quarter comeback wins

First QB to defeat the other 31 teams in the regular season

115 regular season wins as a starting QB in a decade

124 regular and postseason wins as a starting QB in a decade

12 seasons with at least 4,000 passing yards

10 games with 40+ pass attempts in a season

13 consecutive seasons with at least 25 touchdown passes

25 regular season games with at least 4 touchdown passes

8 career games (including 1 playoff game) with at least 5 touchdown passes

5 career games with at least 5 touchdown passes and no interceptions

Conclusion

I hope this book was able to help you to gain inspiration from the life story of Peyton Manning, one of the best players currently playing in the National Football League.

The rise and fall of a star is often the cause for much wonder. But most stars have an expiration date. In football, once a star player reaches his mid- to late-thirties, it is often time to contemplate retirement. What will be left in people's minds about that fading star? In Peyton Manning's case, people will remember how he led one team to another in their journey towards the Super Bowl. He will be remembered as the guy who plucked his team from obscurity, helped them build their image, and honed his own image along the way.

Manning has also inspired so many people because he is the star who never failed to look back, who paid his dues forward by helping thousands of less-fortunate youth find their inner light through sports and education.

Another thing that stands out in Peyton Manning's story is the fact that he never forgot where he came from. As soon as he had the capacity to give back, he poured what he had straight back to those who needed it, and he continues to do so to this day.

Peyton Manning is one of the most captivating talents in football today. Noted for his ability to impose his will on any game, he is a joy to watch on the football field. At the same time, he is one of the nicest guys outside the gridiron, willing to help out teammates and give back to fans. Last but not least, he's remarkable for remaining simple and firm with his principles in spite of his immense popularity.

Other Football Stories That Will Inspire You!

Tom Brady
http://www.amazon.com/dp/B00HJYQTRS

Aaron Rodgers
http://www.amazon.com/dp/B00HJUEDEI

Colin Kaepernick
http://www.amazon.com/dp/B00IRHHABU

Russell Wilson
http://www.amazon.com/dp/B00HK909C8

Calvin Johnson
http://www.amazon.com/dp/B00HJK0YS2

Inspirational Basketball Stories!

Stephen Curry
http://www.amazon.com/dp/B00HH9QU1A

Derrick Rose
http://www.amazon.com/dp/B00HH1BE82

Blake Griffin
http://www.amazon.com/dp/B00INNVVIG

Carmelo Anthony
http://www.amazon.com/dp/B00HH9L3P8

Chris Paul
http://www.amazon.com/dp/B00HIZXMSW

Paul George
http://www.amazon.com/dp/B00IN3YIVI

Dirk Nowitzki
http://www.amazon.com/dp/B00HRVPD9I

Kevin Durant
http://www.amazon.com/dp/B00HIKDK34

Other Inspirational Stories!

Mike Trout
http://www.amazon.com/dp/B00HKKCNNU

Miguel Cabrera
http://www.amazon.com/dp/B00HKG3G1W

Buster Posey
http://www.amazon.com/dp/B00KP11V9S

Lou Gehrig
http://www.amazon.com/dp/B00KOZMONW

Babe Ruth
http://www.amazon.com/dp/B00IS2YB48

Floyd Mayweather
http://www.amazon.com/dp/B00HLEX5O6

Anderson Silva
http://www.amazon.com/dp/B00HLBOVVU

CPSIA information can be obtained
at www.ICGtesting.com
Printed in the USA
LVOW04s2156110216

474785LV00028B/613/P

9 781508 427339